FEB 12 2014

TOP HITS OF 2013

D1298172

BLURRED LINES 2
Robin Thicke feat. T.I. + Pharrell

CALL ME MAYBE 18
Carly Rae Jepsen

CATCH MY BREATH 22
Kelly Clarkson

CRUISE 11
Florida Georgia Line

DAYLIGHT 28
Maroon 5

GET LUCKY 44
Daft Punk featuring
Pharrell Williams

GONE, GONE, GONE 50
Phillip Phillips

HEART ATTACK 58
Demi Lovato

I WILL WAIT 35
Mumford & Sons

IT'S A BEAUTIFUL DAY 64
Michael Bublé

JUST GIVE ME A REASON 72
P!nk featuring
Nate Ruess

MIRRORS 81
Justin Timberlake

NEXT TO ME 96
Emeli Sandé

RADIOACTIVE 100
Imagine Dragons

STAY 112
Rihanna

TRY 118
P!nk

WE CAN'T STOP 105
Miley Cyrus

WHEN I WAS YOUR MAN 124
Bruno Mars

ISBN 978-1-4803-5487-6

HAL•LEONARD® CORPORATION
7777 W. Bluemound Rd. P.O. Box 13819 Milwaukee, WI 53213

For all works contained herein:
Unauthorized copying, arranging, adapting, recording, Internet posting, public performance, or other distribution of the printed music in this publication is an infringement of copyright. Infringers are liable under the law.

Visit Hal Leonard Online at
www.halleonard.com

BLURRED LINES

Words and Music by PHARRELL WILLIAMS
and ROBIN THICKE

© 2013 EMI APRIL MUSIC INC., MORE WATER FROM NAZARETH and I LIKE 'EM THICKE MUSIC
All Rights for MORE WATER FROM NAZARETH Controlled and Administered by EMI APRIL MUSIC INC.
All Rights Reserved International Copyright Secured Used by Permission

G
If you can't hear what I'm try'n' to say, if you can't read
D
from the same page, may-be I'm go-in' deaf, may-be I'm go-in' blind,
C
Bm
Am
G
may-be I'm out of my mind.
O-kay, now he was close,
tried to do-mes-ti-cate ya.
But you're an an-i-mal;
ba-by, it's in your na-ture.

D
Just let me lib - er - ate ya, you don't need no pa - pers. That man is not your mak - er,
C Bm Am G
and that's why I'm gon' take ya, good girl. I know you want it,
I know you want it, I know you want it. You're a good girl.
D
Can't let it get past me. You're far from plas - tic. Talk a - bout get - tin' blast - ed.
C Bm Am
I hate these

G
blurred lines.
I know you want it,
I know you want it,
D
I know you want it. You're a good girl.
The way you grab me,
To Coda
C
Bm
Am
G
must wan-na get nas-ty.
Go a-head, get at me.
What do they make dreams for
when you got them jeans on?
What do we need steam for?
You the hot-test bitch in this place.

D
I feel so luck - y, hey, hey, hey. You wan - na hug me, hey, hey, hey. What rhymes with hug me? Hey, hey,
D.S. al Coda
C
Bm
Am
hey.
CODA
G
Rap: (See additional lyrics)
D
C
Bm
Am

G
Shake your rump, get down. Get up, ah.
D
Do it like it hurt, like it hurt. What? You don't like
C
Bm
Am
G
work?
Ba - by, can you breathe?
I got this from Ja - mai - ca. It al - ways works for me, Da - ko - ta to De - ca - tur.

D
No more pre-tend-in', hey, hey, hey, 'cause now you win-nin', hey, hey, hey. Here's our be-gin-nin', hey, hey,
C
Bm
Am
G
hey. I al-ways want-ed a good girl. I know you want it,
I know you want it, I know you want it. You're a good girl.
D
Can't let it get past me. You're far from plas-tic. Talk a-bout get-tin' blast-ed.
C
Bm
Am
I hate these

G
blurred lines.
I know you want it,
I know you want it,
D
I know you want it. You're a good girl.
The way you grab me,
C
Bm
Am
G
must wan-na get nas-ty.
Go a-head, get at me.
Ev-'ry-bod-y get up.
Ev-'ry-bod-y get up.
Hey, hey,

Additional Lyrics

Rap: One thing I ask of you, let me be the one you back that ass to.
Yo, from Malibu to Paribu, yeah, had a bitch, but she ain't bad as you.
So, hit me up when you pass through, I give you something big enough to tear your ass in two.
Swag on 'em even when you dress casual. I mean, it's almost unbearable.
In a hundred year, not dare would I pull a Pharcide bitch, you pass me by.
I'm nothing like your last guy, he too square for you. He don't smack that ass and pull your hair for you.
So I'm just watchin' and waitin' for you to salute the truly pimpin'.
Not many women can refuse this pimpin'. I'm a nice guy, but don't get it confused, you gettin' it.

CRUISE

Words and Music by CHASE RICE,
TYLER HUBBARD, BRIAN KELLEY,
JOEY MOI and JESSE RICE

Copyright © 2012 Sony/ATV Music Publishing LLC, Dack Janiels Publishing, Big Loud Mountain, Big Red Toe, Deep Fried Dreams and Artist Revolution Publishing
All Rights on behalf of Sony/ATV Music Publishing LLC and Dack Janiels Publishing Administered by Sony/ATV Music Publishing LLC, 8 Music Square West, Nashville, TN 37203
All RIghts on behalf of Big Loud Mountain, Big Red Toe and Deep Fried Dreams Administered by Big Loud Bucks
International Copyright Secured All Rights Reserved

F
Gm
3fr
E♭
3fr
Yeah, when
B♭
F
I first saw that bi - ki - ni top on her, she's
sip - pin' on South - ern and sing - in' Mar - shall Tuck - er. We were
Gm
3fr
E♭
3fr
pop - pin' right out - ta the South Geor - gia wa - ter. Thought: Oh,
fall - in' in love in the sweet heart of sum - mer. She
B♭
F
good Lord! She had them long, tanned legs. Could - n't
hopped right up in - to the cab of my truck and said,

Gm
3fr
E♭
3fr
𝄋
B♭
help my - self, so I walked up and said:
"Fire it up, let's go get this thing stuck."
Well, ba - by, you a song. You
F
Gm
3fr
E♭
3fr
make me wan - na roll my win - dows down and cruise down a
B♭
F
Gm
3fr
back road, blow - in' stop signs through the mid - dle ev - 'ry lit - tle farm town with
E♭
3fr
B♭
F
you in this brand - new Chev - y with a lift kit. Would look a

Gm
3fr
E♭
3fr
B♭
hell of a lot bet - ter with you up in it. So, ba - by, you a song. You
F
Gm
3fr
E♭
3fr
To Coda
make me wan - na roll my win - dows down and cruise.
1
B♭
F
Gm
3fr
E♭
3fr
Well, she was
2
B♭
F
Gm
3fr
E♭
3fr

B♭
F
Gm
E♭
3fr
When that
B♭
F
Gm
sum - mer sun fell to his knees, I looked at her and she
E♭
B♭
F
looked at me and I turned on those K - C lights and drove
Gm
E♭
all night 'cause it felt so right. Her and I, man, we felt

B♭
F
so right. I put it in park and grabbed my gui - tar and strummed
Gm
3fr
E♭
3fr
B♭
a cou - ple chords and sang from the heart. Girl, you sure got the
F
Gm
3fr
E♭
3fr
beat in my chest bump - in'. Hell, I can't get you out - ta my head.
B♭
F
Gm
3fr
Ba - by, you a song. You make me wan - na roll my win - dows down and

E♭
B♭
F
cruise down a back road, blow - in' stop signs through the mid - dle ev - 'ry
Gm
E♭
D.S. al Coda
lit - tle farm town with you. Well,
CODA
B♭
F
Gm
E♭
B♭
Get those win-dows down and cruise.
F
Gm
E♭
B♭

CALL ME MAYBE

Words and Music by CARLY RAE JEPSEN,
JOSHUA RAMSAY and TAVISH CROWE

Copyright © 2011 UNIVERSAL MUSIC CORP., JEPSEN MUSIC PUBLISHING, BMG GOLD SONGS, CROWE MUSIC INC. and BMG PLATINUM SONGS
All Rights for JEPSEN MUSIC PUBLISHING Controlled and Administered by UNIVERSAL MUSIC CORP.
All Rights for BMG GOLD SONGS, CROWE MUSIC INC. and BMG PLATINUM SONGS Administered by BMG RIGHTS MANAGEMENT (US) LLC
All Rights Reserved Used by Permission

Dsus
Csus2
Dsus
but now you're in my way.
it, but it's in my way.
Your stare was hold - in'; ripped jeans, skin was show - in'.
Csus2
Dsus
C
G
Hot night, wind was blow - in'. Where you think you're go - in', ba - by? Hey, I just met you,
D
Em
C
G
D
and this is cra - zy, but here's my num - ber, so call me may - be.
C
G
D
Em
C
G
It's hard to look right at you, ba - by. But here's my num - ber,

D
C
G
D
Em
so call me may-be. Hey, I just met you, and this is cra - zy,
C
G
D
C
G
but here's my num-ber, so call me may-be. And all the oth - er boys
D
Em
C
G
D
try to chase me. But here's my num-ber, so call me may-be.
C
G
D
Em
C
G
Be-fore you came in - to my life, I missed you so bad, I missed you so bad,

D C G D Em
I missed you so, so bad. Be - fore you came in - to my life, I missed you so bad.
To Coda
C G D C G D Em
And you should know that
And you should know that,
I missed you so, so bad.
C G D C G D Em
It's hard to look right at you, ba -
C G D
- by. But here's my num - ber, so call me may - be.
D.S. al Coda
(no repeat)
CODA
D G
so call me may - be.

CATCH MY BREATH

Words and Music by KELLY CLARKSON,
JASON HALBERT and ERIC OLSON

Copyright © 2012 Smelly Songs, Chrysalis One Music, Dejanovas Music and Winona Drive Productions
All Rights for Smelly Songs Administered by Kobalt Songs Music Publishing
All Rights for Chrysalis One Music and Dejanovas Music Administered by BMG Rights Management Ltd. a BMG Chrysalis company
All Rights Reserved Used by Permission

g as written both times.

E
F♯m
E/G♯
life, I won't be told what's sup-posed to be right.
D
E
D
Catch my breath, no one can hold me back. I ain't got time for that.
E
D
E
Catch my breath, won't let 'em get me down.
D
1
E
2
E
It's all so sim-ple now. Ad-dict-ed to the love

D
E
F♯m
D
You helped me see
E
F♯m
D
E
F♯m
the beau - ty in
Esus
N.C.
D
E
F♯m
ev - 'ry - thing. Catch-ing my breath, let-ting it go, turn-ing my
D
F♯m
E
D
E
F♯m
cheek for the sake of the show. Now that you know this is my life, I won't be

Esus
E
D
told what's sup-posed to be right. Catch-ing my breath, let-ting it
(Vocal ad lib. 2nd time)
E
F♯m
E/G♯
go, turn-ing my cheek for the sake of this show. Now that you
D
E
F♯m
know, this is my life, I won't be told what's sup-posed to be
E/G♯
D
E
right. Catch my breath, no one can hold me back.

D
E
D
I ain't got time for that.
Catch my breath,
E
D
1
E
won't let them get me down.
It's all so sim-ple now.
It's all so sim-ple now.
Catch-ing my
2
E
D
E
F♯m
D
E

DAYLIGHT

Words and Music by ADAM LEVINE,
MAX MARTIN, SAM MARTIN
and MASON LEVY

Copyright © 2012 by Universal Music - Careers, Sudgee Music, MXM Music AB, Artist Publishing Group West, Sam Martin Music Publishing and Mason Levy Productions
All Rights for Sudgee Music Administered by Universal Music - Careers
All Rights for MXM Music AB Administered by Kobalt Songs Music Publishing
All Rights for Artist Publishing Group West, Sam Martin Music Publishing and Mason Levy Productions Administered by WB Music Corp.
International Copyright Secured All Rights Reserved

G
Bm
G
but it's late and I'm try - ing not to sleep.
D
G
Bm
'Cause I know when I wake I will have
G
to slip a - way. And when the day -
D
Bm
G
- light comes I'll have to go, but to - night I'm gon - na hold you so

D
Bm
close. 'Cause in the day - light we'll be on our own, but to - night
G
D
I need to hold you so close. Oh. Oh.
Bm
G
D
Oh. Oh.
Bm
G
Oh. Oh.

D
Dsus2
To Coda
Here I am star - ing at your per - fec - tion
D
Dsus2
D
in my arms, so beau - ti - ful. The sky is get - ting light,
Dsus2
D
Dsus2
the stars are burn - ing out. Some - bod - y slow it down. This is way
D
G
Bm
too hard, 'cause I know when the sun

G
D
G
comes up I will leave. This is my last glance

Bm
G
D.S. al Coda
that will soon be mem - o - ry. And when the day -

CODA
A
Bm
G
I nev - er want-ed to stop be-cause I don't want to start all o - ver, start

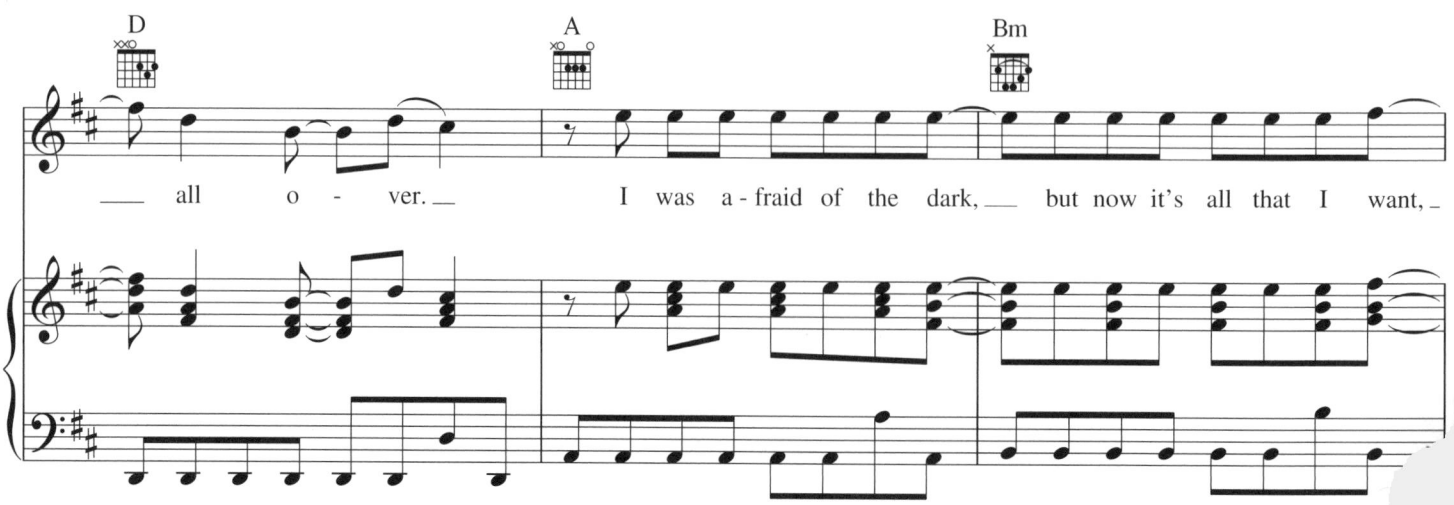
D
A
Bm
all o - ver. I was a - fraid of the dark, but now it's all that I want,

G
all that I want, all that I want.
D
Bm
And when the day - light comes I'll have to go, but to - night
G
D
I'm gon - na hold you so close. 'Cause in the day - light we'll be on
Bm
G
1
D
our own, but to - night I need to hold you so close. And when the day -

2
D
Bm
close.
Oh.
Oh.
Oh.
G
D
Oh.
Oh.
Bm
G
1
D
Oh.
Oh.
2
D

I WILL WAIT

Words and Music by
MUMFORD & SONS

Copyright © 2012 UNIVERSAL MUSIC PUBLISHING LTD.
All Rights in the U.S. and Canada Controlled and Administered by UNIVERSAL - POLYGRAM INTERNATIONAL TUNES, INC.
All Rights Reserved Used by Permission

D
and I fell heav -
will blow a - way
Asus
- y in - to your arms.
with this new sun.
1
2
Bm
These days of
But I'll
I'll
A/C♯
D
G(add2)
D/F♯
kneel down, wait for
kneel down, know my

A
D
now.
ground.
And
And I will wait, I
F♯m
A(add4)
will wait for you.
And
D
Dmaj7/F♯
I will wait, I will wait for you.
A(add4)
D
1

2
D
So break my step
seen
G
and re - lent.
and him with less.
You for -
Now in some
D
gave
way
and I won't
shake the ex -
Asus
for - get.
cess.
1
Know what we've

2
D
'Cause I will wait, I
F♯m
will wait for you.
Asus
D
And I will wait, I
F♯m
will wait for you.
1
Asus
And

2
Asus
D
Now I'll be bold
G
as well as strong and use my
D
Asus
head a - long - side my heart.
D
So take my flesh and fix my

G
D
eyes,
a teth - ered
mind
Asus
free
from the
lies.
Bm
A/C♯
D
G(add2)
I'll
kneel
down,
wait
I'll
kneel
down,
know
D/F♯
1
A
2
A
for
now.
my
ground.

D
A/C♯
Bm
G
D/F♯
A
D
A/C♯
Raise my
bow my
Bm
G
D/F♯
hands,
head,
paint my spir - it
keep my heart

1
2
A
A
gold. And slow. 'Cause
D
F♯m
I will wait, I will wait for you.
Asus
D
And I will wait, I will wait for you.
F♯m
Asus
D
1st time: And

GET LUCKY

Words and Music by THOMAS BANGALTER,
GUY MANUEL HOMEM CHRISTO, PHARRELL WILLIAMS
and NILE RODGERS

Copyright © 2013 Imagem CV, EMI April Music Inc., More Water From Nazareth and XLC Music
All Rights for More Water From Nazareth Controlled and Administered by EMI April Music Inc.
All Rights for XLC Music Administered by Sony/ATV Music Publishing LLC, 8 Music Square West, Nashville, TN 37203
All Rights Reserved Used by Permission

Bm
D
- ning? Uh, the force from the be - gin -
- ing? If you wan - na leave, I'm read -
F♯m
E
- ning.
- y.
𝄋 Bm
D
We've come too far to give up
F♯m
E
who we are. So

Bm
D
F♯m
let's raise the bar and our cups to the stars.
E
Bm
She's up all night 'til the sun.
D
F♯m
I'm up all night to get some.
She's up all night for good fun.
E
Bm
I'm up all night to get luck - y.
We're up all night 'til the sun.

D
F♯m
We're up all night to get some.
We're up all night for good fun.
E
Bm
We're up all night to get luck - y.
We're up all night to get luck - y.
D
F♯m
We're up all night to get luck - y.
We're up all night to get luck - y.
1
E
D.C.
We're up all night to get luck - y.
2, 3
E
To Coda
We're up all night to get luck - y.

Bm
D
We're up all night to get luck - y.
We're up all night to get luck - y.
F♯m
E
We're up all night to get luck - y.
We're up all night to get luck - y.
Bm
D
We're up all night to get luck - y.
We're up all night to get luck - y.
F♯m
1
E
We're up all night to get luck - y.
We're up all night to get luck - y.

2
E
D.S. al Coda
(take 2nd ending)
We're up all night to get luck - y.
CODA
Bm
We're up all night to get luck - y.
D
We're up all night to get luck - y.
F♯m
We're up all night to get luck - y.
E
We're up all night to get luck - y.
Bm
D
F♯m
E
Repeat and Fade
Opt. Ending
Bm

GONE, GONE, GONE

Words and Music by GREGG WATTENBERG,
DEREK FUHRMANN and TODD CLARK

*Recorded a half step higher.

© 2012 EMI APRIL MUSIC INC., G WATT MUSIC, EGG SONGS PUBLISHING and AE FUHRMANN PUBLISHING
All Rights for G WATT MUSIC Controlled and Administered by EMI APRIL MUSIC INC.
All Rights Reserved International Copyright Secured Used by Permission

Dm7
shut down the cit - y lights, I'll lie, cheat, I'll beg and bribe to
B♭sus2
make you well, to make you well. When
F5
en - e - mies are at your door, I'll car - ry you a - way from war if
fall like a sta - tue, I'm gon' be there to catch you, put you
Csus
3fr
you need help, if you need help. Your
on your feet, you on your feet. And if

Dm7
hope dan - gling by a string, I'll share in your suf - fer - ing to
your well is emp - ty, not a thing will pre - vent me. Tell me
B♭(add2)
3fr
make you well, to make you well. Give me
what you need. What do you need? I sur -
B♭ F C B♭ F
rea - sons to be - lieve that you would do the same for
ren - der hon - est - ly; you've al - ways done the same for
C N.C. B♭ F
me. And I will do it (for you, for
me. So

Dm7
C
B♭
F
you.)
Ba - by, I'm not mov - ing on, I'll love you long
af - ter you're gone.
(For you, for
you.)
You will nev - er sleep a - lone; I'll love you long
1
N.C.
af - ter you go, and long af - ter you're gone, gone,

F5
gone.
When you
2
N.C.
Dm7
F
long af - ter you're gone, gone, gone. You're my back - bone, you're my cor - ner - stone,
B♭sus2
B♭(add2)
3fr
Dm7
you're my crutch when my legs stop mov - ing. You're my head start,
F
B♭sus2
you're my rug - ged heart, you're the pulse that I've

B♭(add2)
3fr
B♭sus2
F
Dm7
Csus
3fr
al - ways need - ed. Like a drum, ba - by, don't stop beat - in'.
B♭sus2
F
Dm7
Csus
3fr
B♭sus2
F
Like a drum, ba - by, don't stop beat - in'. Like a drum, ba - by,
Dm7
Csus
3fr
B♭sus2
F
Dm7
Csus
3fr
don't stop beat - in'. Like a drum, my heart nev - er stops beat - in' (for
B♭
F
Dm7
C
B♭
F
you, for you.) Ba - by, I'm not mov-ing on, I'll love you long

Dm7
C
B♭
F
af - ter you're gone. (For you, for
Dm7
C
1
B♭
F
you.) You will nev - er sleep a - lone; I'll love you long
Dm7
C
2
B♭
F
af - ter you go. (For nev - er sleep a - lone; I'll love you long,
Dm7
C
N.C.
long af - ter you go. Like a drum, ba - by,

don't stop beat - in'. Like a drum, ba - by, don't stop beat - in'.
Like a drum, ba - by, don't stop beat - in'. Like a drum, my heart
F5
F/A
G7sus
nev - er stops beat - in' for you. And long af - ter you're gone, gone,
F5
F5
F/A
G7sus
F5
gone, I'll love you long af - ter you're gone, gone, gone.
rit.

HEART ATTACK

Words and Music by JASON EVIGAN, MITCH ALLAN,
SEAN DOUGLAS, NIKKI WILLIAMS, AARON PHILLIPS
and DEMI LOVATO

Copyright © 2013 BMG PLATINUM SONGS, BAD ROBOT, PART OF THE PROBLEM, ART IN THE FODDER MUSIC,
SWEET GRASS COUNTY MUSIC, INTERNATIONAL DOG MUSIC, a division of BIG YELLOW DOG LLC, SEVEN PEAKS MUSIC and DEMI LOVATO PUBLISHING
All Rights for BMG PLATINUM SONGS and BAD ROBOT Administered by BMG RIGHTS MANAGEMENT (US) LLC
All Rights for PART OF THE PROBLEM and ART IN THE FODDER MUSIC Administered by BUG MUSIC, INC., a BMG CHRYSALIS COMPANY
All Rights for SWEET GRASS COUNTY MUSIC Administered by WB MUSIC CORP.
All Rights for DEMI LOVATO PUBLISHING Administered by SEVEN PEAKS MUSIC
All Rights Reserved Used by Permission

D♭ A♭ E♭ Fm
Nev-er had trou-ble get-ting what I want. But when it comes to you, I'm nev-er good e-nough.
And ev-'ry time I try to be my-self, it comes out wrong like a cry for help.
D♭ A♭ E♭ Fm
When I don't care, I can play him like a Ken doll.
It's just not fair, pain's more trou-ble than love is worth.
D♭ A♭ E♭ Fm
Won't wash my hair, then make 'em bounce like a bas-ket-ball.
I gasp for air. It feels so good, but you know it hurts.
D♭ A♭ E♭ Fm
But you make me wan-na act like a girl, paint my nails and wear high
But you make me wan-na act like a girl, paint my nails and wear per-

D♭
A♭
4fr
C7
N.C.
heels. Yes, you make me so nerv-ous that I just can't hold your hand.
fume. For you make me so nerv-ous that I just can't hold your hand.
You make me
𝄋
D♭
A♭
4fr
E♭
3fr
Fm
glow, but I cov - er up. Won't let it
D♭
A♭
4fr
E♭
3fr
show. So I'm
D♭
Cm
3fr
Fm
B♭m
put - tin' my de - fens - es up 'cause I don't wan - na fall in love. If I

Db/Ab
4fr
N.C.
To Coda
Fm
Db
ev - er did that, I think I'd have a heart at - tack.
Ab
4fr
Eb
3fr
1
Fm
Db
I think I'd have a heart at - tack.
Ab
4fr
Eb
3fr
I think I'd have a heart at - tack.
2
Fm
Db
tack.
Ab
4fr
Eb
3fr
Fm
I think I'd have a heart at - tack. The feel - ings got

D♭
A♭
4fr
lost in my lungs; they're burn - ing. I'd rath - er be numb. And there's
E♭
3fr
Fm
no one else to blame. So scared, I take
D♭
A♭
4fr
off in a run. I'm fly - ing too close to the sun, and I burst in - to
C7
D.S. al Coda
flames. You make me

CODA
Fm
Db
Ab
4fr
Eb
3fr
tack.
I think I'd have a heart at -
tack.
I think I'd have a heart at - tack -
tack.
I think I'd have a heart at -
tack.
I think I'd have a heart at - tack.

IT'S A BEAUTIFUL DAY

Words and Music by MICHAEL BUBLÉ,
ALAN CHANG and AMY FOSTER

© 2013 WB MUSIC CORP., I'M THE LAST MAN STANDING MUSIC, INC., WARNER-TAMERLANE PUBLISHING CORP., IHAN ZHAN MUSIC and SONGS FROM THE HEATLEY CLIFF
All Rights for I'M THE LAST MAN STANDING MUSIC, INC. Administered by WB MUSIC CORP.
All Rights for IHAN ZHAN MUSIC Administered by WARNER-TAMERLANE PUBLISHING CORP.
All Rights for SONGS FROM THE HEATLEY CLIFF Administered by SONGS OF KOBALT MUSIC PUBLISHING
All Rights Reserved Used by Permission

D♭
A♭
4fr
B♭m
Ba - by, it's fine you said that we should just be friends; well, I came
G♭
D♭
A♭
4fr
up with that line, and I'm sure that it's for the best. And if you ev - er
B♭m
G♭
B♭m
change your mind, don't hold your breath. 'Cause you may
F+
3
F7
B♭m
not be - lieve, mm, that, ba - by,
3

F+
F7
I'm re - lieved.
When you
E♭m7
6fr
A♭
4fr
said good - bye, my whole world shined.
Hey, hey, hey.
D♭
A♭(add4)
6fr
B♭m
It's a beau - ti - ful day, and I can't stop my - self from smil -
A♭(add4)
6fr
G♭
D♭
- ing. If we're drink - ing, then I'm buy - ing.
And I know

G♭
D♭
A♭
4fr
D♭
there's no de - ny - ing, it's a beau - ti - ful day;
A♭(add4)
6fr
B♭m
A♭(add4)
6fr
the sun is up, the mu - sic's play - ing. And e - ven
G♭
D♭
G♭
if it start - ed rain - ing, you won't hear this boy com-plain -
D♭
G♭
F7
To Coda
- ing, 'cause I'm glad that you're the one who got a - way.

B♭m
A♭
D♭
It's a beau - ti - ful day.
D♭
A♭
It's my turn to fly. So, girls, get in line,
B♭m
G♭
A♭
G♭/B♭
A♭/C
D♭
'cause I'm eas - y; no play - ing this guy like a fool. 'Cause now I'm al -
A♭
B♭m
G♭
A♭/G♭
G♭maj7
A♭/G♭
right; you might-'ve had me caged be - fore, but not to - night. And

B♭m
F+
F7
you may not be - lieve, mm, that,
B♭m
F+
ba - by, I'm re - lieved.
F7
G♭
A♭
4fr
This fire in - side, it burns too
G♭maj7
bright. I don't wan - na say "so long"; I just wan - na

A♭
4fr
say
"good - bye."
D♭
A♭(add4)
6fr
It's a beau - ti - ful day,
and I can't stop
D.S. al Coda
CODA
B♭m
A♭
4fr
'Cause if you ev - er think I'll take up my time with
G♭5
D♭5
4fr
think - ing of our break - up, then you've got an - oth - er thing
G♭

F7/A
3fr
B♭m
A♭5
4fr
com - ing your way.
'Cause it's a beau - ti - ful
D♭
A♭
4fr
B♭m
day.
G♭maj7
D♭
A♭
4fr
Beau - ti - ful day.
Oh, ba - by, an - y day that you're
B♭m
G♭
D♭/F
E♭m
6fr
E♭m/A♭
6fr
D♭
gone a - way,
it's a beau - ti - ful day.
3
3
rit.

JUST GIVE ME A REASON

Words and Music by ALECIA MOORE,
JEFF BHASKER and NATE RUESS

© 2012 EMI BLACKWOOD MUSIC INC., PINK INSIDE PUBLISHING, SONY/ATV MUSIC PUBLISHING LLC, WAY ABOVE MUSIC, WB MUSIC CORP., FBR MUSIC and BEARVON MUSIC
All Rights for PINK INSIDE PUBLISHING Controlled and Administered by EMI BLACKWOOD MUSIC INC.
All Rights for SONY/ATV MUSIC PUBLISHING LLC and WAY ABOVE MUSIC Administered by SONY/ATV MUSIC PUBLISHING LLC, 8 Music Square West, Nashville, TN 37203
All Rights for FBR MUSIC and BEARVON MUSIC Administered by WB MUSIC CORP.
All Rights Reserved International Copyright Secured Used by Permission

C G Em Bm/D A/C♯
ev - 'ry touch, you fixed them. Now you've been talk - ing in your
D Dsus Em Bm/D A/C♯ D Dsus
sleep, oh, oh, things you nev - er say to me, oh, oh.
Em Bm/D A/C♯ D G/B C G/B
Tell me that you've had e - nough of our love, our
Dsus D G D/F♯
love. Just give me a rea - son, just a lit - tle bit's e - nough, just a

Em
Bm/D
C
Bm
D7sus
sec - ond. We're not bro - ken, just bent, and we can learn to love a - gain.
G
D/F♯
Em
Bm/D
C
Bm
It's in the stars. It's been writ - ten in the scars on our hearts: we're not bro - ken, just bent,
D7sus
G
and we can learn to love a - gain.
Male: I'm
C
Em
sor - ry. I don't un - der - stand where all of this is com - ing from. I

C
G
thought that we were fine.
Your
Female: Oh, we had ev - 'ry - thing.
C
Em
head is run - ning wild a - gain. My dear, we still have ev - 'ry - thing, and
C
G
it's all in your mind. Female: Yeah, but this is hap - pen - ing.
Em
Bm/D
A/C♯
D
Dsus
Em
Bm/D
A/C♯
Male:
You've been hav - ing real bad dreams, oh, oh. You used to lie so close to

D
Dsus
Em
Bm/D
A/C♯
D
G/B
Both:
me, oh, oh. There's noth - ing more than emp - ty sheets be - tween our
C
G/B
Am
C
G/B
3
Female: love, our
love, our love, Male: oh, our love, our
3
Dsus
D
G
D/F♯
love.
love.
Both: Just give me a rea - son, just a lit - tle bit's e - nough, just a
Em
Bm/D
C
Bm
D7sus
sec - ond. We're not bro - ken, just bent, and we can learn to love a - gain.

G
D/F♯
Em
Bm/D
C
Bm
Male:
I nev - er stopped: you're still writ - ten in the scars on my heart.
Both:
You're not bro - ken, just bent,
D7sus
Em
Bm
and we can learn to love a - gain.
Female: Oh, tear ducts and rust.
Male: I'll fix it for us.
C
D
Em
Female:
We're col - lect - ing dust, but our love's e - nough.
Male:
You're hold - ing it in.
Bm
C
G/B
Am
Female:
You're pour - ing a drink.
Male:
Now noth - ing is as bad as

D
N.C.
it seems. Female: We'll come clean. Both: Just give me a rea-son, just a
lit - tle bit's e - nough, just a sec - ond. We're not bro - ken, just bent,
and we can learn to love a - gain. It's in the stars. It's been
writ - ten in the scars on our hearts, that we're not bro - ken, just bent,

G
D/F♯
and we can learn to love a - gain. Just give me a rea - son, just a lit - tle bit's e - nough, just a
Em
Bm/D
C
Bm
D7sus
sec - ond. We're not bro - ken, just bent, and we can learn to love a - gain.
G
D/F♯
It's in the stars. It's been writ - ten in the scars on our hearts,
Em
Bm/D
C
Bm
D7sus
that we're not bro - ken, just bent, and we can learn to love a - gain.

G
D/F♯
Em
Bm/D
C
Bm
Female: Oh, we can learn to love a - gain. Oh,
D7sus
G
D/F♯
we can learn to love a - gain. Oh,
Em
Bm/D
C
Bm
D7sus
Em
Bm/D
A/C♯
that we're not bro - ken, just bent, and we can learn to love a - gain.
D
G/B
C
G/B
Am
G5
3fr

MIRRORS

Words and Music by JUSTIN TIMBERLAKE,
JAMES FAUNTLEROY, JEROME HARMON,
TIM MOSLEY, CHRIS GODBEY and GARLAND MOSLEY

Copyright © 2013 by Universal Music - Z Tunes LLC, Tennman Tunes, Almo Music Corp., Underdog West Songs, Fauntleroy Music,
Warner-Tamerlane Publishing Corp., Jerome Harmon Productions, WB Music Corp., Virginia Beach Music, B Max Entertainment Publishing and 757 Music
All Rights for Tennman Tunes Administered by Universal Music - Z Tunes LLC
All Rights for Underdog West Songs and Fauntleroy Music Controlled and Administered by Almo Music Corp.
All Rights for Jerome Harmon Productions Administered by Warner-Tamerlane Publishing Corp.
All Rights for Virginia Beach Music Administered by WB Music Corp.
International Copyright Secured All Rights Reserved

Cm
3fr
Gm
3fr
Fm
- thing to ad - mi - re? 'Cause your shine is some-thing like a mir -
- thing, an or - i - gi - nal, 'cause it does - n't seem mere - ly as - sem -
A♭
4fr
Cm
3fr
Gm
3fr
- ror, and I can't help but no - tice you re - flect in this heart of mine.
- bled. And I can't help but stare, 'cause I see truth some-where in your eyes.
Fm
G/B
Cm
3fr
If you ev - er feel a - lone
I can't ev - er change with - out
Gm
3fr
Fm
A♭
4fr
and the glare makes me hard to find, just know that I'm al -
you. You re - flect me; I love that a - bout you. And if I could

Cm
3fr
Gm
3fr
Fm
- ways par - al - lel on the oth - er side.
I would look at us all the time.
G/B
Cm
3fr
Gm
3fr
'Cause with your hand in my hand and a pock - et full of soul, I can tell you there's no
Fm
A♭
4fr
Cm
3fr
place we could-n't go. Just put your hand on the past, I'll be try'n' to pull you
Gm
3fr
Fm
N.C.
through. You just got - ta be strong. 'Cause I don't wan - na lose you now.

E♭
B♭
A♭
I'm look - ing right at the oth - er half of me. The
E♭
B♭
va - can - cy that sat in my heart is a space that now you hold.
A♭6
E♭
Show me how to fight for now. And I'll
B♭
Fm
Cm
tell you, ba - by, it was eas - y com - ing back here to you once I fig - ured it out.

E♭
3fr
B♭
A♭
4fr
You were right here all a - long.
E♭
3fr
B♭
It's like you're my mir - ror, oh, my mir - ror star - ing back
A♭
4fr
E♭
3fr
at me. I could - n't get an - y big - ger, oh,
B♭
A♭
4fr
with an - y - one else be - side of me. And now, it's clear as this prom -

E♭
3fr
B♭
Fm
- ise that we're mak - ing, two re - flec - tions in - to one.
Cm
3fr
E♭
3fr
B♭
'Cause it's like you're my mir - ror, oh, my mir - ror star - ing back
A♭
4fr
To Coda
1
G/B
2
at me, star - ing back at me. Aren't you some - at me.
Fm
Cm
3fr
Yes - ter - day is

Fm
his - to - ry, oh;
Cm
3fr
B♭
Fm
to-mor - row's a mys-ter - y, oh.
Cm
3fr
A♭
4fr
I can see you look - ing back at me. Keep your eyes on me,
D.S. al Coda
N.C.
ba - by, keep your eyes on me. 'Cause I don't wan - na lose you now.

CODA
E♭
B♭
at me. Oh.
A♭6
E♭
Oh.
B♭
A♭
E♭
Oh, oh.
B♭
Fm
Cm
E♭
Ooh.

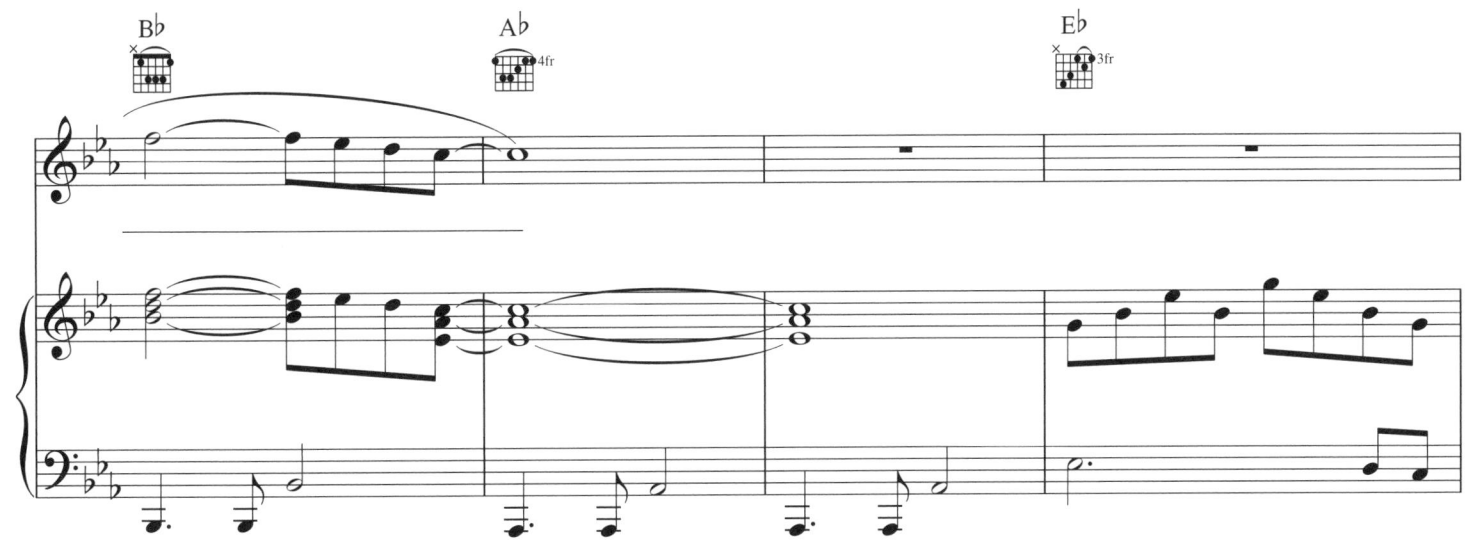
B♭
A♭
4fr
E♭
3fr

B♭
A♭
4fr
E♭
3fr

B♭
A♭
4fr
E♭
3fr

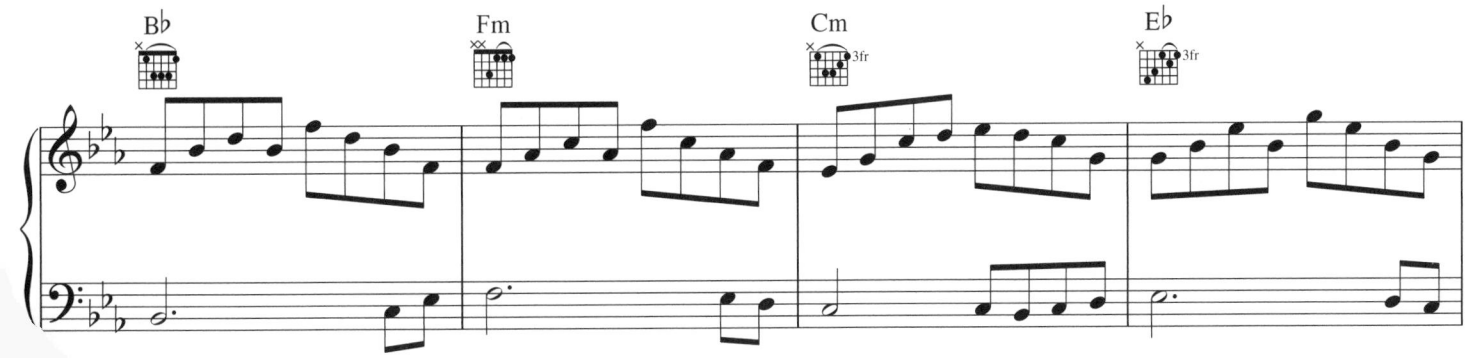
B♭
Fm
Cm
3fr
E♭
3fr

B♭
A♭
4fr
N.C.
You are, you are
Cm
3fr
the love of my life. You are, you are the love of my life.
Oh.
Gm
3fr
Fm
Cm
3fr
Oh.
Gm
3fr
Fm
Cm
3fr
Oh, oh.

Gm
Fm
Cm
3fr
Ooh.
Now, you're the in - spi - ra - tion
for this pre - cious song.
And I just wan - na see your face light
up since you put me on.
So now I say good - bye to the old me;

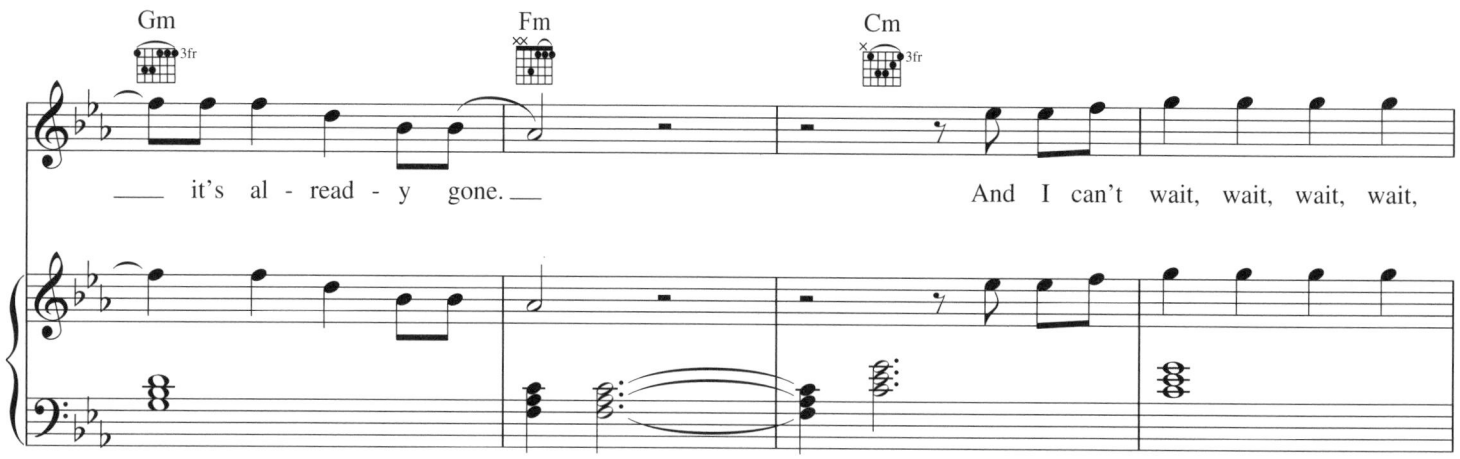
Gm
3fr
Fm
Cm
3fr
it's al - read - y gone.
And I can't wait, wait, wait, wait,

Gm
3fr
Fm
Cm
3fr
wait to get you home,
just to let you know, you are...

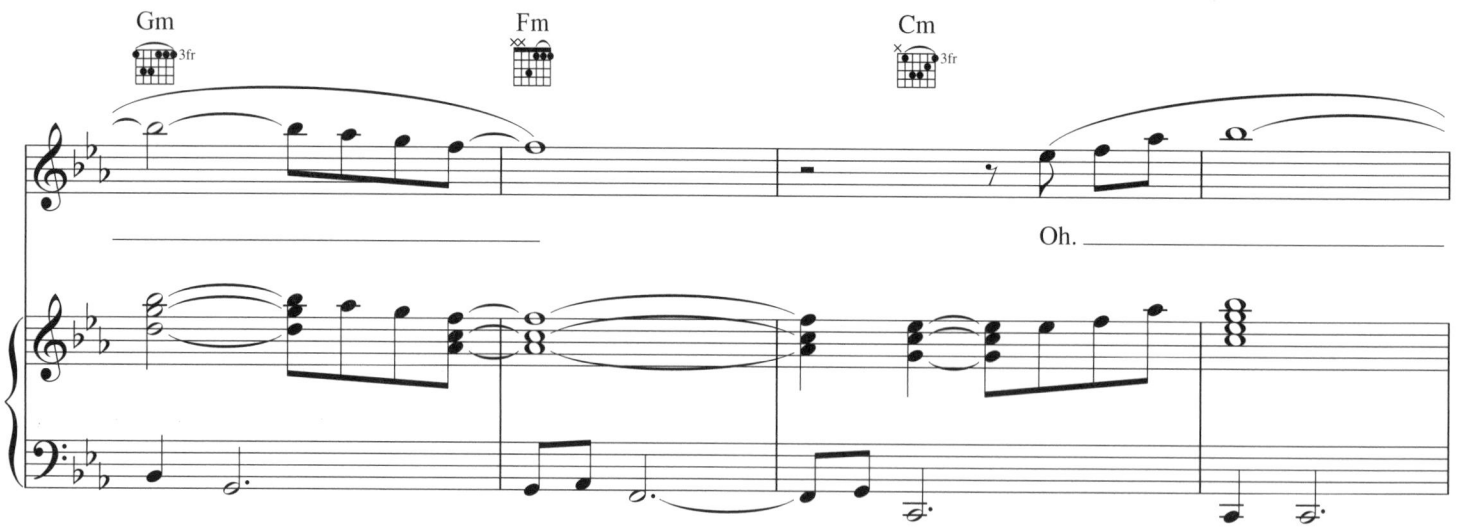
Gm
3fr
Fm
Cm
3fr
Oh.

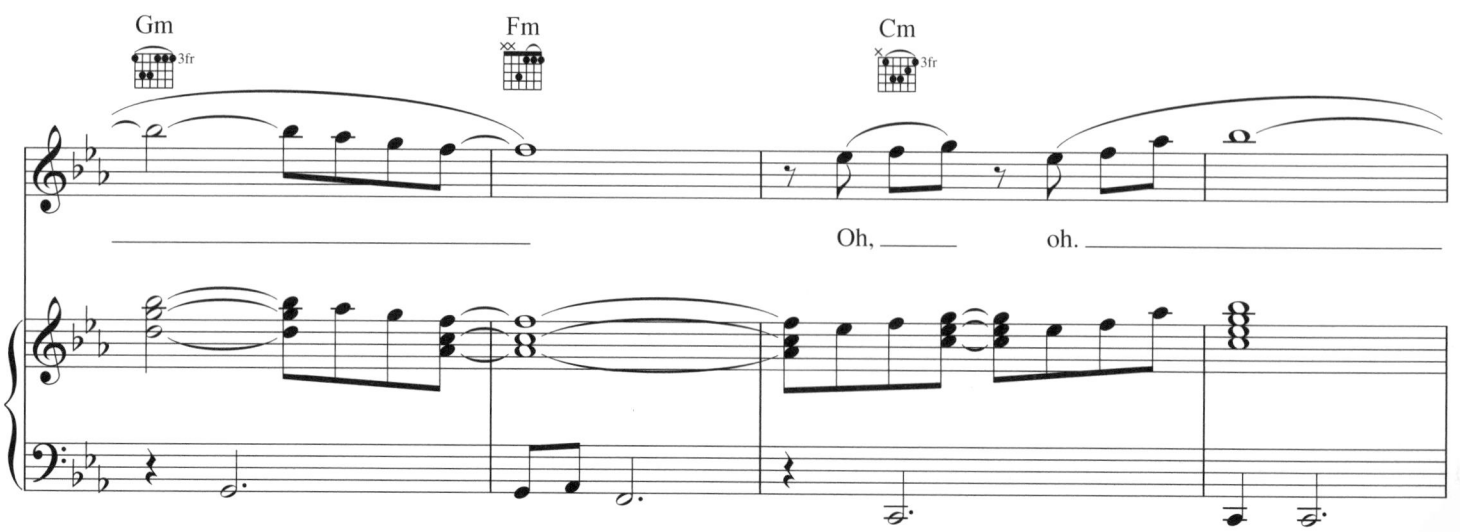
Gm
3fr
Fm
Cm
3fr
Oh,
oh.

Gm
Fm
Cm
3fr
Ooh.
Girl, you're my re - flec - tion,
all I see is you.
My re - flec - tion
in ev - 'ry - thing I do.
You're my re - flec - tion

Gm
3fr
Fm
Cm
3fr
and all I see is you.
My re - flec - tion
Gm
3fr
Fm
Cm
3fr
in ev - 'ry - thing I do.
Oh.
Gm
3fr
Fm
Cm
3fr
Oh.
Gm
3fr
Fm
Cm
3fr
Oh, oh.

Gm
Fm
Cm
3fr
Ooh.
You are, you are
the love of my life. You are, you are the love of my life. You are, you are
the love of my life. You are, you are the love of my life. the love of my life.
1
2

NEXT TO ME

Words and Music by EMELI SANDÉ,
HARRY CRAZE, HUGO CHEGWIN
and ANUP PAUL

© 2012 STELLAR SONGS LTD, SONY/ATV MUSIC PUBLISHING UK LIMITED, NAUGHTY WORDS LIMITED and ANUP PAUL PUBLISHING DESIGNEE
All Rights for STELLAR SONGS LTD. in the U.S. and Canada Controlled and Administered by EMI BLACKWOOD MUSIC INC.
All Rights for SONY/ATV MUSIC PUBLISHING UK LIMITED and NAUGHTY WORDS LIMITED Administered by SONY/ATV MUSIC PUBLISHING LLC, 8 Music Square West, Nashville, TN 37203
All Rights Reserved International Copyright Secured Used by Permission

Am
G/B
C
him, you'll find him next to me.
him, I'll find him next to me.
When the
Am
G/B
C
You won't find him try'n' to chase the dev - il for
skies are grey and all the doors are clos - ing, and the
end has come and build - ings fall - ing down fast, when we
Am
G/B
C
mon - ey, fame, for pow - er out of greed.
ris - ing pres - sure makes it hard to breathe, when all I
spoiled the land and dried up all the sea, when
3
Am
G/B
C
You won't nev - er find him where the rest go. You will find
need's a hand to stop the tears from fall - ing, I will find
ev - 'ry - one has lost their heads a - round us, you will find

Am
G/B
C
him, you'll find him next to me.
him, I'll find him next to me.
him, you'll find him next to me.
Next to me,
Am
G/B
C
Am
G/B
ooh, next to me, ooh,
C
Am
G/B
C
ooh. Next to me, ooh, ooh.
You will find
I will find
You will find
To Coda
1
Am
G/B
C
him, you'll find him next to me.
him, I'll find him next to me.
him, you'll find him next to me.
When the

2
C
D.S. al Coda
When the
CODA
C
Next to me,
Am
G/B
C
ooh, next to me, ooh,
Am
G/B
C
Am
G/B
C
ooh. Next to me, ooh, ooh, you will find
Am
G/B
C
him, you'll find him next to me.
N.C.

RADIOACTIVE

Words and Music by DANIEL REYNOLDS,
BENJAMIN McKEE, DANIEL SERMON,
ALEXANDER GRANT and JOSH MOSSER

Copyright © 2012 SONGS OF UNIVERSAL, INC., IMAGINE DRAGONS PUBLISHING, ALEXANDER GRANT and JMOSSER MUSIC
All Rights for IMAGINE DRAGONS PUBLISHING and ALEXANDER GRANT Controlled and Administered by SONGS OF UNIVERSAL, INC.
All Rights Reserved Used by Permission

to ash and dust; I wipe my
and dye my clothes. It's a rev - o -
brow and I sweat my rust. I'm breath - ing in
lu - tion, I sup - pose. We're paint - ed red
the chem - i - cals.
to fit right in.
Gasping inhale...
Whoa,
...exhale.
whoa.
Play 2nd time only
Bm
D
I'm break - ing in
and shap - ing up,
Play both times

A
E5
then check - ing out on the pris - on bus.
Bm
D
A
This is it, the A - poc - a - lypse. Whoa,
N.C.
Bm
D
whoa.
I'm wak - ing up. I feel it in my bones, e -
A
E5
Bm
nough to make my sys - tems blow. Wel - come to the new age,

D
A
E/G♯
to the new age. Wel-come to the new age, to the new age.
Bm
D
A
Whoa, oh. Whoa, I'm ra-di-o-ac-tive,
E5
Bm
D
ra-di-o-ac-tive. Whoa, oh. Whoa, I'm
Asus2
To Coda
1
N.C.
ra-di-o-ac-tive, ra-di-o-ac-tive.

2
N.C.
ra - di - o - ac - tive. All sys - tems go;
the sun has - n't died.
Deep in my bones, straight from in - side...
D.S. al Coda
...I'm wak - ing
CODA
N.C.
ra - di - o - ac - tive.

WE CAN'T STOP

Words and Music by MILEY CYRUS,
MICHAEL WILLIAMS, PIERRE SLAUGHTER,
TIMOTHY THOMAS, THERON THOMAS,
DOUGLAS DAVIS and RICKY WALTERS

© 2013 Tondolea Lane Music Publishing, WB Music Corp., Sounds From Eardrummers LLC, Warner-Tamerlane Publishing Corp., Eardrummers Music Publishing LLC,
Pierre Slaughter Publishing Designee, Universal Music Corp., T.N.T. Explosive Publishing, Entertaining Music and Slick Rick Music Corp.
All Rights for Tondolea Lane Music Publishing Administered by Seven Summits Music
All Rights for Sounds From Eardrummers LLC Administered by WB Music Corp.
All Rights for Eardrummers Music Publishing LLC and Pierre Slaughter Publishing Designee Administered by Warner-Tamerlane Publishing Corp.
All Rights for T.N.T. Explosive Publishing Controlled and Administered by Universal Music Corp.
All Rights Reserved Used by Permission

C♯m
4fr
Asus2
'cause we came to have so much fun now.
Bet some-bod-y here might get some now.
E
G♯m
4fr
If you're not read-y to go home,
can I get a hell no?
C♯m
4fr
Asus2
'Cause we gon-na go all night 'til we see the sun-light, al-right.
So,
𝄋
E5
G♯5
4fr
la, da, dee, da, dee, we like to par-ty.
Danc-in' with Mi-ley, do-in' what-ev-er we

C♯5
4fr
A5
5fr
want.
This is our house, this is our rules. And we can't
E
G♯m
4fr
stop.
And we won't
stop.
Can't you see it's
C♯m
4fr
Asus2
we who own the night? Can't you see it's we who 'bout the life? And we can't
E5
G♯5
4fr
stop.
And we won't
stop.
We run

C♯5
4fr
A5
5fr
things, they don't run we. Don't take noth - in' from no - bod - y, yeah, yeah.
E
G♯m7
4fr
It's our par - ty, we can do what we want. It's our par - ty, we can say what we want.
C♯m7
4fr
Asus2
To Coda
It's our par - ty, we can love who we want. We can kiss who we want. We can screw who we want.
E
G♯m
4fr
To my home girls here with the big butt, shak - in' it like we at a strip club,

C♯m
4fr
Asus2
re-mem-ber, on-ly God can judge ya. For-get the hat-ers,'cause some-bod-y loves ya.
E
G♯m
4fr
And ev-'ry-one in line in the bath-room, try'n' a get a line in the bath-room.
C♯m
4fr
Asus2
D.S. al Coda
We all so turned up here, get-tin' turned up, yeah, yeah, yeah. So,
CODA
E5
G♯5/D♯
11fr
It's our par-ty, we can do what we want to.
It's our house, we can love who we want to.

C♯5
4fr
A5
5fr
It's our song, we can sing if we want to.
It's my mouth, I can say what I want to, yeah,
E5
G♯5/D♯
11fr
yeah,
yeah,
C♯5
4fr
A5
5fr
yeah,
eh.
And we can't
E
G♯m
4fr
stop.
And we won't stop.
Can't you see it's

C♯m
4fr
Asus2
we who own the night? Can't you see it's we who 'bout the life? And we can't
E
G♯m
4fr
C♯m
4fr
stop. And we won't stop. We run things, they don't run we. Don't take
Asus2
E
G♯m
4fr
noth-in' from no-bod-y, yeah, yeah. Yeah, yeah,
C♯m
4fr
Asus2
N.C.
eh.

STAY

Words and Music by MIKKY EKKO
and JUSTIN PARKER

Copyright © 2012 Sony/ATV Music Publishing LLC, Sony/ATV Music Publishing UK Limited and Kkids And Stray Dogs
All Rights Administered by Sony/ATV Music Publishing LLC, 8 Music Square West, Nashville, TN 37203
International Copyright Secured All Rights Reserved

C
Dm
Am
Am7
Am
Am7
hands in the air, said, "Show me some - thin'."
It's not much of a life you're liv - in'.
Am
Am7
C
Dm
Am
Am7
He said, "If you dare, come a lit - tle clos - er."
It's not just some - thin' you take; it's giv - en.
Am
Am7
Am
F6
'Round and a - round and a -
Dm
Am
round and a - round we go.
Oh,

F6
Dm
G
now, tell me now, tell me now, tell me now you know.
C
Dm
Not real - ly sure how to feel a - bout it. Some -
Am
F
C
- thin' in the way you move makes me feel like I can't
Dm
Am
To Coda
F
live with - out you. Well, it takes me all the way, I want you to stay.

1
C
Dm
Am
Am7
Am
Am7
Am
Am7
2
C
Dm
Am
Am7/G
5fr
Am
Am7/G
5fr
Am
F
Ooh,
Am
Dm
Em
the rea - son I hold on,

F
Am
Dm
ooh, 'cause I need this hole gone.
F
Fun - ny you're the bro - ken one but I'm the on - ly one who need - ed
Am
Dm
sav - in'. 'Cause when you nev - er see the light, it's
F
G
Gsus
3fr
D.S. al Coda
hard to know which one of us is cav - in'.

CODA
F
C
Dm
I want you to stay,
Am
F
C
stay.
Dm
Am
F
I want you to stay,
C
Dm
Am
F
ooh.

TRY

Words and Music by busbee
and BEN WEST

Copyright © 2010 BMG Platinum Songs, Hello I Love You Music and Legitimate Efforts Music
All Rights Administered by BMG Rights Management (US) LLC
All Rights Reserved Used by Permission

Bm G D A5 Bm G
Some-times I think that it's bet - ter to nev - er ask why.
D A5 Bm G D A5
Bm G D G
Where there is de - sire, there is gon - na be a
D A Bm
flame. Where there is a flame, some-one's bound to get burned. But just be-cause it

G
D
A
burns does-n't mean you're gon-na die; you got-ta get up and try and try and
Bm
G
D
try, got-ta get up and try, and try, and try, got-ta get up
A
Bm
G
D
A
Bm
G
and try, and try, and try.
D
A5
5fr
B5
Bm
G
D
A5
5fr
Fun-ny, how the heart can be de-ceiv-ing
Ev-er wor-ry that it might be ru-ined?
And

Bm G D A5 B5 Bm G
more than just a cou - ple times.
Why do we fall in love so
does it make you wan - na cry?
When you're out there do - ing what you're
D A5 Bm G 1 D A5 B5
eas - y,
e - ven when it's not right?
do - ing,
are you just get - ting by?
2 D A5 Bm G D
Tell me, are you just get - ting by, by, by? Where there is de -
G D A5
sire, there is gon - na be a flame.
Where there is a flame, some - one's bound to get

Bm
G
D
burned. But just be-cause it burns does-n't mean you're gon-na die; you got-ta get up
A
Bm
G
and try and try and try, got-ta get up and try and try,
D
A
1
Bm
try. You got-ta get up and try and try, try, got-ta get up
2
Bm
G
D
try, you got-ta get up and try and try, try. You got-ta get up

A Bm G D A
and try and try and try.
Bm G D A5 5fr B5 Bm G
You got - ta get up and try and try and
D A Bm G(♭5) 3fr D A5 5fr
try, got - ta get up and try, try, try.
Bm G D A5 5fr Bm G(♭5) 3fr D Asus Bm

WHEN I WAS YOUR MAN

Words and Music by BRUNO MARS,
ARI LEVINE, PHILIP LAWRENCE
and ANDREW WYATT

© 2012 BMG GOLD SONGS, MARS FORCE MUSIC, UNIVERSAL MUSIC CORP., TOY PLANE MUSIC, NORTHSIDE INDEPENDENT MUSIC PUBLISHING LLC,
THOU ART THE HUNGER, WB MUSIC CORP., ROC NATION MUSIC, MUSIC FAMAMANEM and DOWNTOWN DMP SONGS
All Rights for BMG GOLD SONGS and MARS FORCE MUSIC Administered by BMG RIGHTS MANAGEMENT (US) LLC
All Rights for TOY PLANE MUSIC Controlled and Administered by UNIVERSAL MUSIC CORP.
All Rights for THOU ART THE HUNGER Administered by NORTHSIDE INDEPENDENT MUSIC PUBLISHING LLC
All Rights for ROC NATION MUSIC and MUSIC FAMAMANEM Administered by WB MUSIC CORP.
All Rights for DOWNTOWN DMP SONGS Administered by DOWNTOWN MUSIC PUBLISHING LLC
All Rights Reserved Used by Permission

Dm
G
me down,
I've made,
'cause my heart breaks a lit - tle when I hear
and it haunts me ev - 'ry time I close
C
Em/B
Am
Em
your name.
my eyes.
It all just sounds like, "Ooh,
hoo."
Mm,
B♭
C/G
G
too young, too dumb to re - al - ize
that I should-'ve bought you flow-
F
G
C
- ers and held your hand;
should - 've gave you all my hours

F
G
C
when I had the chance; take you to ev - 'ry par -
F
G
Am
D7
- ty, 'cause all you want - ed to do was dance.
Now my ba - by's danc -
8vb
F
Fm
1
C
F
- ing, but she's danc - ing with an - oth - er man.
C
Em/B
2
C
F
Al - though it hurts, I'll be the

G
C
G/B
Am
Em/G
first to say that I was wrong. Oh, I
D7
Dm7
know I'm prob-'ly much too late to try and a - pol - o - gize for my mis - takes, but I just want
G
N.C.
you to know, I hope he buys you
F
G
C
flow - ers; I hope he holds your hand, give you all his

F
G
C
hours when he has the chance; take you to ev - 'ry par -
F
G
Am
D7
- ty, 'cause I re - mem - ber how much you love to dance; do all the things I
F
Fm
C
D7
should-'ve done when I was your man. Do all the things I
F
Fm
C
should - 've done when I was your man.
rit.